PETER THE LITTLE SUNFLOWER

Written by Susan Kinnane

Illustrated by Janie Kinnane

Written by Susan Kinnane
Illustrations by Janie Kinnane

Photograph of Susan Kinnane by Maureen Azize
Photograph of Janie Kinnane by Sarah Petrarca

Published by Miriam Laundry Publishing Company
miriamlaundry.com

HC ISBN 978-1-998816-71-2
PB ISBN 978-1-998816-57-6
e-Book ISBN 978-1-998816-58-3

FIRST EDITION

To Mama Mary
Thank you Jay, for telling me that Mary was my Mother. It forever made a huge difference in my life.
Thank you, Josie
For Wednesdays

Peter was waking up.

He didn't want to leave the warmth of his bed, deep in the farmer's field, but something was calling to him.

What is that? wondered Peter. Being curious, he just had to peek. Wiggling and squirming, Peter finally poked his head out of the ground.

"Good morning!" the Sun called cheerfully.

"Good morning!" shouted Peter. "I'm here!"

"Yes, you are, Peter!" laughed the Sun.

"Hey, how did you know my name?"
Peter asked.

"We all know your name," replied the Sun.
"We've been waiting for you."

"We?" Peter looked around. To his joy, he found himself surrounded by his family, and they were all happy to see him.

Each day Peter grew taller and stronger, until one day, his petals opened to the Sun!

It seemed that Peter couldn't keep his head from turning as the Sun moved across the sky.

"Why do I move my head with the Sun, Mommy?" asked Peter.

"You are seeking the Sun's light," explained his mother. "That light gives you the energy you need to grow."

Now Peter understood who had been calling him to wake up. It was the Sun! "I love it when the Sun is in my face," he giggled. "It makes me happy all over."

His mother said, "The Sun is important. It is the center of our lives."

At the end of the day, Peter watched the Sun as it silently set in the West and all was quiet in the farmer's field. Throughout the night, Peter's face slowly turned back towards the East, ready for the Sun to rise again.

Each morning, Peter couldn't wait to see his friend. "Good Morning, Sun!" he called out excitedly as the Sun arrived.

"Good Morning, Peter!" the Sun joyfully called back.

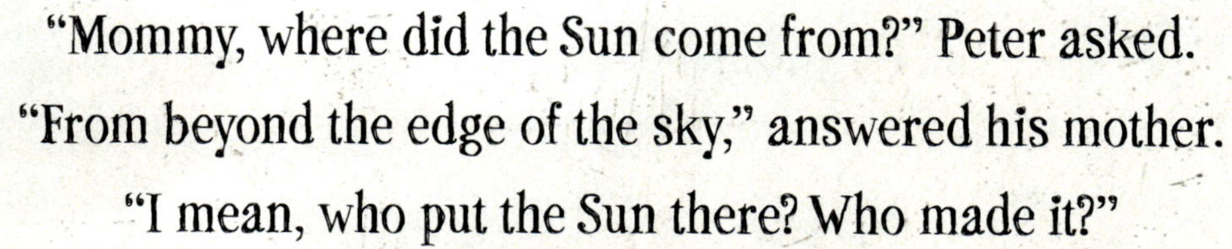

"Mommy, where did the Sun come from?" Peter asked.

"From beyond the edge of the sky," answered his mother.

"I mean, who put the Sun there? Who made it?"

"God did," his mother replied.

"How about me? Who made me?"

"God made you, too, Peter," said his mother.

"But why?"

"Because he loves you."

Peter nodded. "I feel loved."

"That's because you belong to God," his mother said.

A big smile came across Peter's face. "Mommy, does God have a son, like you have me?

"Yes, Peter. God's Son is Jesus. He is Light and Love."

"Does Jesus have a mommy like I have you?"

Peter's mother nodded. "Her name is Mary. She brings all of us to know Jesus because she loves all of us unconditionally."

"Unconditionally? What does that mean?"

His mother smiled. "It means we are her children, and she loves us no matter who we are."

Peter pondered all these things in his heart.

There was a family that lived on this lovely little farm. Every weekday Peter watched as they came to work in the field and pick the sunflowers to take to market. On Saturdays, they chose flowers to decorate the Church.

"Mommy, what happens to us after we are picked?" asked Peter.

"We bring joy to all those who see us," answered his mother.

"After that, what happens, Mommy?"

"This beautiful field is our temporary home, Peter. Soon, we will go to our forever home with God."

One day, Papa gathered all the children around him.
Peter paid very close attention.
"Children, all this is a gift from God," Papa said.

"Then we should give Him a gift back," laughed one of the children. "I think I will give myself to God."

"If you make Him the center of your life, that's the perfect gift," said Papa gently.

One of the children found a blue wildflower amongst the sunflowers. "How pretty!" she exclaimed. "Can I pick this one to decorate the Church?"

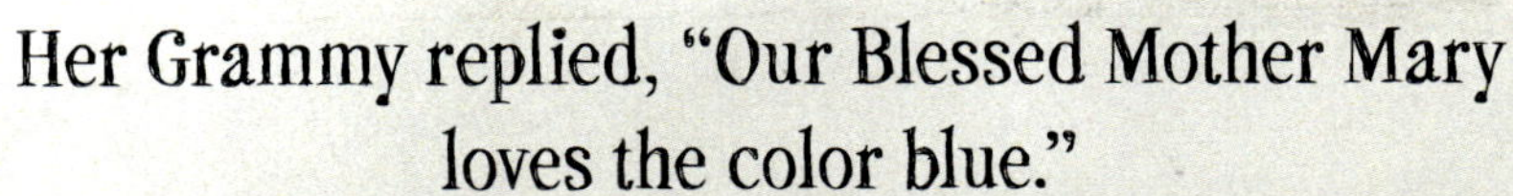

Her Grammy replied, "Our Blessed Mother Mary loves the color blue."

"Then I will pick it for my Mama Mary in Heaven," the little girl said joyfully.

Mama Mary in Heaven, thought Peter.

He liked that name best of all. *Maybe next time they bring flowers to the Church for Mama Mary, they will bring me!*

Just like the farmer, Peter found great joy in his life and the things happening around him. He drank in the warm, gentle breezes that blew and tickled Peter's petals and made him dance in the wind. He laughed as the butterflies bounced across the field and delighted in the grasshoppers, ladybugs, beetles, and ants.

The changing colors of the sky, and the ocean with all its wonders, made Peter stand in silent awe.

Peter even loved the bees that buzzed about his petals, whispering to him their secrets of the day. "Are you telling me that today is the day I get picked to decorate the Church?" whispered Peter.

But none of these joys compared to the sweet joy the Sunrise held for him each day.

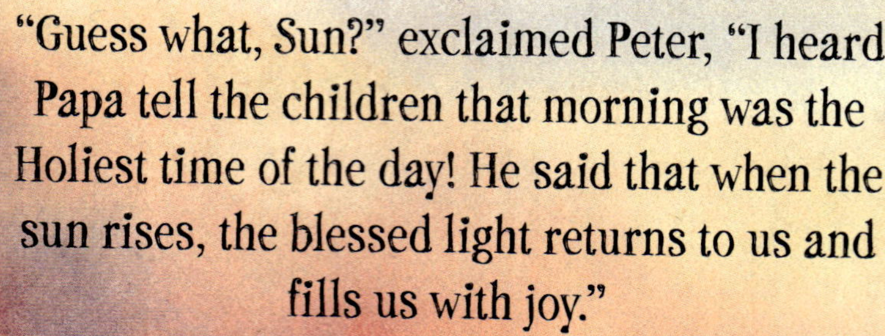

"Guess what, Sun?" exclaimed Peter, "I heard Papa tell the children that morning was the Holiest time of the day! He said that when the sun rises, the blessed light returns to us and fills us with joy."

Just as he was saying this, Peter saw the farmer walking towards him. "Oh my goodness," he squealed. "It's today! Today is the day I am picked!"

But the farmer walked past Peter and picked other sunflowers.

Peter drooped. He wondered, *Why not me?*

Only the best sunflowers were chosen and brought to market. Peter knew he wasn't one of those! Why, he wasn't even as tall as his brothers and sisters! *Should I be worried?* he wondered.

Just as Peter was about to ask the Sun, the Sun disappeared behind some angry clouds. The wind came out of nowhere, and rain fell from the sky.

"What's happening?" Peter shouted.

The rain came down so hard, it hurt as it hit him. Peter was violently pushed around by the wind and soaked by the rain. "How long will this last?" Scared, he cried out, but no one could hear him.

Am I abandoned?

At last the storm ended. Peter was lying in the field, covered in mud. The storm had tossed him around, crushed his leaves, and a couple of petals were missing!

"There's no way I will be picked now," Peter softly cried. The thought of it made him wilt, right where he lay.

Suddenly, Peter could hear laughter. The children were coming into the field.

"Oh, look," said the youngest. "The poor thing." Very gently they took Peter by the stem and stood him up. "Now he's perfect again!"

Peter was confused. He was bruised and broken, and yet the children found him perfect.

Then he remembered Mama Mary's unconditional love.
Imagine! To be loved and to belong just the way he was!

The last clouds blew away and the Sun appeared.

Something began to happen inside of Peter. He felt as if the light of the Sun was filling him with warmth and joy. He straightened up and decided that he would be the best little sunflower he could be, just the way he was!

He turned his beautiful face to the Sun.

The very next Saturday, the youngest of the farm children made her way towards Peter. Peter couldn't believe what was happening. He was being picked!

And after bringing joy to all who saw him, Peter went to his forever home with God and Mama Mary in Heaven.

Made in the USA
Middletown, DE
22 June 2023